Fun, Inter
About the Oly....

MW01133198

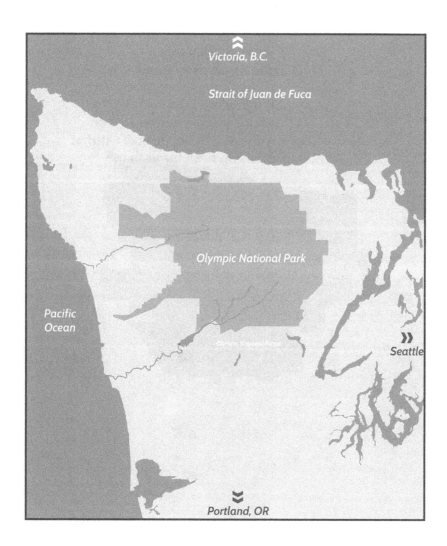

Victoria, B.C.

Strait of Juan de Fuca

Olympic National Park

Pacific
Ocean

Olympic National Forest

Seattle

Portland, OR

Melanie Richardson Dundy
ChildrensBooksByMelanie.com

Copyright © 2021
by Melanie Richardson Dundy

All rights reserved
No part of this book may be reproduced or
transmitted in any form or by any means without
written permission from the author.

MDCT Publishing
Melanie Richardson Dundy
melanie.dundy@icloud.com

Hello

I am Markus. I am an Olympic marmot, and Olympic marmots do not live anywhere in the whole world except on the Washington Olympic Peninsula.

I want to tell you about some really cool things you can find on the peninsula. I will start by telling you about the coolest of all — ME.

Let me try to tell you — in the most modest way I know how — just how special I am. In 2009, Washingtonians chose me as their state animal. So what do you think about that? That is proof positive that I am cool! Right?

Some people affectionately call me a whistle pig because of the high-pitched whistling sound I make to alert my fellow marmots of danger. When I am scared out of my wits, I can even sound like those people who scream in scary movies.

My favorite thing to do is lay on rocks to sun myself in the morning before I hunt for my breakfast. Nothing feels better than the warm sun on my soft, furry belly.

I live in a colony with other Olympic marmots. We spend about 80% of our lives below ground. We spend a lot of time nuzzling and playing with each other.

We marmots like to eat together. Being herbivores, we eat nuts, leaves, seeds, flowers, grass, and grains.

We eat a lot in the summer to store up enough fat to get us through our eight month hibernation.

After hibernation, we try to return to our healthy, chubby, adorable selves.

Now that I have told you about the most amazing and important thing on the Olympic Peninsula — ME, I would like to tell you about some other stuff that you might find really interesting.

Consider me your official guide from here on out.

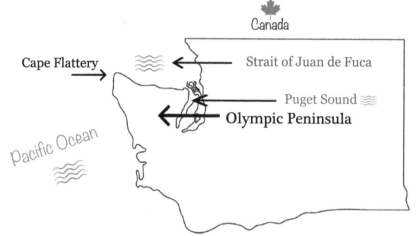

Canada

Cape Flattery

Strait of Juan de Fuca

Puget Sound

Olympic Peninsula

Pacific Ocean

As your official guide, I guess the first thing I should explain is that a peninsula is a piece of land almost surrounded by water or projecting out into a body of water.

The Olympic Peninsula is a 3600 square mile section of land that sticks out of the west side of the state of Washington. It lies across a narrow stretch of water called Puget Sound and is where you will find the Olympic National Park.

Cape Flattery on the Peninsula is the north-westernmost point in the contiguous United States.
(Contiguous United States: the 48 adjoining states. Alaska and Hawaii are not included.)

Some of the last areas ever explored in the contiguous United States are here. No one even made a complete map of the peninsula until 1898.

Canada is just across the Strait of Juan de Fuca. You can actually see Canada from many places on the Washington side of the strait.

Beautiful Olympic National Park

The Olympic National Park covers one million acres of the Olympic Peninsula and is home to wilderness and wildlife seen nowhere else on the face of the earth.

The Olympic Park includes three distinct ecosystems that stretch from the beautiful coast to glacier-capped mountains and from lush, green rainforests and old-growth forests to sprawling meadows.
(Ecosystem: a geographic area where plants, animals, and other organisms, as well as weather and landscape, work together to form a bubble of life.)

The entire Olympic Peninsula is moving and has been moving for the past 50 million years.

So beautiful!

Did you know that there are fish fossils at the very top of the Olympic Mountains?

That is so weird! How did fish get to the top of a mountain?

Well, it makes sense once you realize that the Olympic Mountain Range is not volcanic; but was born in the sea.

Here is what happened: Some 65 million years ago, underwater volcanoes erupted. They gushed red hot lava that cooled into basalt, a volcanic rock, on the ocean floor. This basalt sludge built up and covered the ocean floor like a thick blanket.

But, then the ocean floor shifted causing two HUGE pieces of the earth's crust to collide. This collision formed the Olympic Mountains.

In other words, the Olympic Mountains are a large uplifted and folded section of oceanic crust that moved upward onto the continent over the last 40 million years. The mountains have only been above sea level for about 18 million years.

Confused? Jennifer Natoli, a park ranger, describes it in a way that is easier to understand. Get yourself an Oreo cookie and follow along.

Split an Oreo Cookie in two by twisting it.

Now think of the two cookie halves as two HUGE pieces of the earth's crust that are about to collide.

Pretend the creamy filling on the lower part of the cookie is the layers of basalt blanketing the ocean floor.

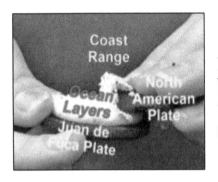

Now, slide the lower cookie beneath the upper cookie so that the creamy filling is scraped into a pile.

This is what happened millions of years ago when one piece of the earth's crust slid over the fine-grained volcanic rock (basalt) on the other piece of the earth's crust. The same way the filling piled up on the cookie, the basalt rock was scraped off the earth's crust and piled up to form the Olympic Mountains.

Uh, oh. I don't think I was supposed to start eating my cookie yet.

Mount Olympus is considered the crown jewel of the Olympic Mountain Range because it is the highest peak in the park (7,980 feet tall). Here is an interesting fact about Mount Olympus: it cannot be seen from Seattle, Tacoma, Olympia, Sequim, or Port Angeles, because it is hidden behind other mountains.

Hurricane Ridge is much easier to visit and the best place to view Mount Olympus and Blue Glacier. On a clear day, from its elevation of 5,242 feet, you get great views of Mount Olympus, Blue Glacier, deer, black bear, and, most importantly, you may get to see me or my marmot friends up close. After all, that is where we live. From there you can also see the Strait of Juan de Fuca and clear across the water into Canada.

Hurricane Ridge is called Hurricane Ridge because of the intense hurricane-strength winds that occur. The weather is so unpredictable, it can be warm and sunny one minute and snowing the next. It can snow any time of the year.

The rangers at the visitor center are really smart. You can ask them any questions you want because they know everything about everything up there.

The Mighty Glaciers

I can't tell you about the Olympic Mountains without talking about the glaciers. A glacier is a slow-moving mass of ice on a mountain. There are 60 named glaciers and over two hundred unnamed glaciers in the Olympic Mountains. Blue Glacier is the park's largest glacier, spilling down Mount Olympus for almost 3 miles.

(Blue Glacier sits on top of Mount Olympus)

During the last Ice Age, which started about 2.6 million years ago and lasted until roughly 11,000 years ago, the park was surrounded on 3 sides with ice 3,500 feet thick. Today, these mountains are the most glaciated area in the United States except for Alaska.

The glaciers that are present today continue to move. Glaciers can grow and advance or shrink and retreat moving the landscape with them. With the current warming climate and more melting periods than freezing periods throughout the year, the glaciers are shrinking and retreating.

All these glaciers that are so important to our environment, *could* very possibly disappear by the end of this century.

We cannot allow that to happen! We need to fight climate change NOW!

Wet, Wet Rainforests

What makes a rainforest? Rain, rain, rain, rain, rain, and moderate temperatures. The Olympic rainforests get 12-14 *feet* of rain per year. And the temperatures rarely fall below freezing or go above 80 degrees.

The park's four rainforests were once part of a much, much larger Pacific Northwest rainforest that stretched all the way from Oregon's southern coast to southeastern Alaska. WOW! That was one BIG rainforest!

Today, the Hoh Rainforest is the wettest place in the lower 48 states and is one of the most untouched, diverse environments in the U.S. It is the most carefully preserved rainforest in the northern hemisphere (the half of the earth that is north of the equator). Its unique ecosystem has remained unchanged for thousands of years, and it is recognized as one of the seven wonders of Washington state.

If you hike in a rainforest, you will see a lot of nurse logs, which are remnants of downed trees. If you take the time to study the nurse logs, you will be surprised to see all the life they support. They provide homes for small animals, growing conditions for seeds and Epiphytes (plants that grow on other plants), and burrowing places for lots of insects.

Quinault Rainforest, another rainforest in the park, has the Valley of the Giants. It is home to six of the world's largest species of evergreens,

including the world's largest Sitka Spruce, which is 1,000 years old, 191 feet tall, and 17.7 feet in diameter.

Vast Olympic Wilderness

Over 95% of Olympic National Park (876.669 acres) is designated wilderness. The entire state of Rhode Island is only 776,957 acres. That means there are 100,000 more acres of wilderness in the Olympic National Park than the entire size of the state of Rhode Island.

I know that's hard to believe, but it's true.

The Olympic National Park protects over 75 miles of wilderness coast and over 4,000 miles of rivers and streams. There are over 20 reptile and amphibian species, 37 native fish species, 300 bird species, 56 mammal species (including 25 marine mammal species), 22 species listed as endangered or threatened, and 1 National Natural Landmark (Point of Arches) pictured below.

Olympic National Park gets over
30 million visitors every year.

Olympic Peninsula Coastline

Is that Gramps viewing that small island? No, I guess that's just a big rock, but it sure looks like my grampa.

The Olympic coast is full of seabirds, rocky headlands, beaches, unusual-looking trees that have been shaped by strong winds, and amazing tide pools.

Tide pools are shallow pools of seawater that exist only at low tide. They are full of plants and animals, some of which make their homes there such as clams, snails, barnacles, and crabs.

There are also the sea anemones. Sea Anemones are half plant, half-animal and dine on the fish, crabs, sea stars, mollusks, and living sand dollars that share the tide pools with them.

Some sea animals are accidentally washed into the tide pools and get stuck there. They have to wait until the next high tide comes and washes them back out to sea.

All these creatures survive the extremes of the changing tides twice a day. Now that's big-time resilience!

Breaching whales can be spotted from the Olympic Peninsula beaches between April and May when they are migrating north and then again between October and November when the whales are migrating south.

Be a Junior Ranger

Olympic National Park Ocean Stewards Junior Ranger program is a fun, hands-on program for children ages four and up. As an Ocean Steward you will explore the coastal ecosystem of Olympic National Park, learn exciting new facts about this unique ecosystem, and understand how you can help protect Olympic National Park's wilderness coast and ocean.

Pick up your copy at any visitor center when you arrive. Complete the book according to the instructions to receive your Ocean Steward patch.

www.nps.gov/olym/learn/kidsyouth/beajuniorranger.htm

Banana Slugs

I'll bet you can guess why they are called banana slugs.

Banana slugs are very important to the Olympic National Park's ecosystem. They eat organic debris and vegetation and then they spread the seeds. You might say banana slugs serve as composters for the park. Another cool fact about banana slugs is they reproduce all on their own. No mate is needed. No dating or falling in love with another banana slug is necessary.

I have to tell you, though, these guys produce a lot of yucky, defensive mucus which explains why banana slugs have no natural predators. If an animal was to try to eat one of these slugs, it would get a mouthful of very slippery slug plus a lot of slippery slime. The banana slug's icky slime will make an enemy's tongue or throat go numb. Any curious animal that dares to poke or prod the banana slug with its nose or tongue will quickly discover that the slime acts as an anesthetic. *YUCK!*

Some people believe kissing a banana slug will bring good luck. Do you think that is something you might want to try?

*The truth is that even a small peck from you could transfer harmful bacteria to the slug's organs. So even if you wanted to kiss a slug, slugs will definitely **not** want to kiss you.*

Time Machine Anyone?

Everything I have told you about up until now has been about the living, breathing world of the Olympic Peninsula. That's because that's the only world I, as a marmot, have experienced.

But, I recently heard about something really strange that exists in the material world of the peninsula.

Have you ever heard of an underground town? Would you like to see and explore one? Believe it or not, the town of Port Angeles has one.

Going into these underground tunnels is like getting into a time machine and going back 100 years.

In 1914, the people of Port Angeles were so worried their town might flood that they decided it would be a great idea to elevate their streets over the town. This decision created an entire underground world connected by a series of tunnels. There were businesses, stores, even a theater, entirely under the streets.

People, *but not marmots*, can still explore the actual tunnels and buildings to get a taste of life in another century and what it would be like to live on another level.

Come to think of it, I guess I already know what it's like to live on another level.

Holy, Moly! It's A Mastodon

Farmer Manis lived on a farm on the Olympic Peninsula near Sequim. He walked out of his house one August morning in 1977 with the intention of digging a fish pond on his property. Well, believe it or not, he ended up digging up two 8-foot long mastodon tusks. At first, he thought they were just some old logs. Can you imagine how shocked he must have been to find out they were mastodon tusks?

Not only did Farmer Manis find the bones of a mastodon, but he found bones of a mastodon that had a 13,800 year-old spearhead stuck in its rib. The spearhead had been made from a bone of a completely *different mastodon.*

X-rays determined the injury from the spearhead healed after just 3 to 4 months. The mastodon went on to live to the ripe old age of 45. It died of natural causes according to scientists who studied the wear on the teeth and the arthritic condition of the mastodon's bones.

The tusks and bones of the mastodon had been preserved in the wet ground for 13,000 to 14,000 years. There were cuts and scratches on the bones which indicated the mastodon had been butchered for food after it had died.

This was an amazing discovery!

Scientists now knew that humans hunted these prehistoric animals on the Olympic Peninsula. In other words, this is the oldest evidence of human life in the Pacific Northwest.

And even more skulls and teeth were found in other areas of Sequim!

(Farmer Manny Manis and his wife, Clare,
holding the mastodon tusks)

The fossil remains of the mastodon are now on display at the Sequim Museum & Arts in Sequim, Washington.
www.sequimmuseum.com

Roosevelt Elk

Roosevelt elk are named after President Theodore Roosevelt, 26th president of the United States and devoted conservationist. (Conservationist: person who acts for the protection and preservation of the environment and wildlife)

The largest wild herd of Roosevelt elk in the Pacific Northwest makes its home in Olympic Park. They are the largest elk in North America. Most females weigh 600 to 700 pounds, but bulls can weigh as much as 1,100 pounds!

Both males and females are beautiful. Their heads are dark brown, and their bodies are pale brown. They have large white rumps and stubby tails.

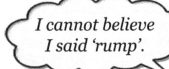

I cannot believe I said 'rump'.

By 1909, the Roosevelt elk herds were getting smaller and were in danger of becoming extinct. President Roosevelt came to their rescue. He created what is now known as Olympic National Park. In other words, he found a way to preserve the native habitat of the elk herds.

Thank you, President Roosevelt!

Absolute Silence

Have you ever experienced absolute silence? You may think you have — like when you are in bed at night or at home by yourself. But is that true silence? If you close your eyes and listen, you will hear something; the refrigerator humming, a dog barking, wind blowing, cars driving by, or maybe a distant train. True silence is almost impossible to experience, and it is something you will never forget once you do experience it.

So where can you find true and complete silence? In the Hoh Rainforest of the Olympic National Park.

One Square Inch of Silence was created on Earth Day in 2005 by researchers of noise pollution. It is on the trail above Mt. Tom Creek Meadows and is marked by a red stone sitting on top of a mossy log. Keep a careful eye out, so you don't miss it.

The creators of One Square Inch of Silence hope that if people have a chance to listen to true, natural silence, they will become more aware of all the noise pollution that exists in the environment. They want us to be aware of and protect one of the most important and endangered resources on the planet — **silence**. Natural quiet is actually in danger of becoming non-existent in our world in the next 10 years.

My marmot buddies and I hiked the trail and found the rock. We now have a new understanding of the word, "silence."

Sasquatch (Big Foot)

It's big! It's hairy! It has terrible body odor!

But is it real? Or, is it a hoax?

Will you be the one to solve the mystery and discover the truth? For hundreds of years, people have reported sightings of big, hairy, smelly, wild creatures living in the Olympic forests.

Self-proclaimed eyewitnesses have described Sasquatch as a big ape-like creature ranging from 6 to 15 feet tall when standing upright. They claim he moves silently but sometimes releases a high-pitched cry.

Sasquatch footprints have measured up to 24 inches in length and 8 inches in width.

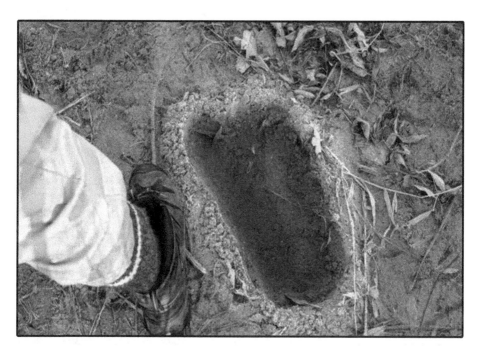

Sasquatch/Big Foot investigators (and there are many) claim the Olympic Peninsula rainforests create the perfect habitat for the creature: rainy climate, tons of cover, water, forest-strewn landscape, and plenty of food.

So listen closely, and be aware of your surroundings when you are hiking on the peninsula. You may just hear or see something when you least expect it.

The Superhero Tree

This tree, located on the Pacific Coast of the peninsula, is one of the most famous trees in the world. It defies all the rules of science and biology. Some call it a freak of nature, some call it the Tree of Life, but my marmot friends and I prefer to think of it as the *Superhero Tree*.

As you can see, the tree sits on a cliff. Years of intense erosion have created a cave exposing the majority of the roots under the tree. (Erosion: the process by which the surface of the earth gets worn down by natural elements such as wind and water.)

So how can the tree continue breathing when its roots travel to nowhere? How can the tree survive all the intense coastal storms when its roots do not hold it in place?

Beyond all logic, our *Superhero Tree* lives on.

The cave is appropriately called *the tree root cave* since its roof is entirely made of roots. People have told me that it was formed by a small stream that slowly washed the soil away from underneath the tree. Decades of erosion have taken the life-giving soil away but have never been able to stop the tree from thriving.

How is the top so green? How has another tree not taken over like so often happens? This tree is amazing! It is still fighting and still breathing.

This *Superhero Tree* is a true example of just how powerful nature really is. Its determined roots are supplying the tree with life even without soil.

If you ever get discouraged about something or feel defeated in any way, take a minute to think about this tree that has never given up.

When you are determined, you will continue to grow too.

Mystery Alert!

100 Gigantic Trees Fall at the Same Time

The tree fall was so massive and strong that it registered as a small earthquake.

These were not just average trees. They were GIGANTIC, HUGE, old-growth trees that were hundreds of years old.

It happened on the north shore of Lake Quinault at 1:30 in the morning on January 27, 2018.

Some of the enormous trees completely fell over while others were snapped like twigs at the base of their trunks.

So what caused it? No one knows for sure, but many scientists, meteorologists, and believers in the supernatural have strong opinions.

Olympic National Park officials believe it was some sort of violent wind event, but this theory makes no sense. Nearby weather stations reported only light breezes on that particular night. Plus, radar indicated that there was not a hint of instability in the air or any kind of storm in the area.

Others believe the destruction may have been caused by an angry Sasquatch/Big Foot, an ugly troll, or maybe even a UFO trying to land.

What do you think happened?

Native American Tribes

"From where and when?"
"Here and always."

The Olympic Peninsula is home to seven Native American Tribes. By the mid to late 1800s, all the tribes had signed treaties with the United States. The treaties recognized the tribes as Sovereign Nations and reserved their right to "hunt, fish, and gather in their usual and accustomed places" forever. Each tribe has the right to govern itself and deal with other tribes and nations on government-to-government basis.

The tribes currently residing on the Washington Olympic Peninsula are:

Jamestown S'Kalllam
Lower Elwha Klallam
Skokomish
Hoh
Makah
Quinault
Quileute

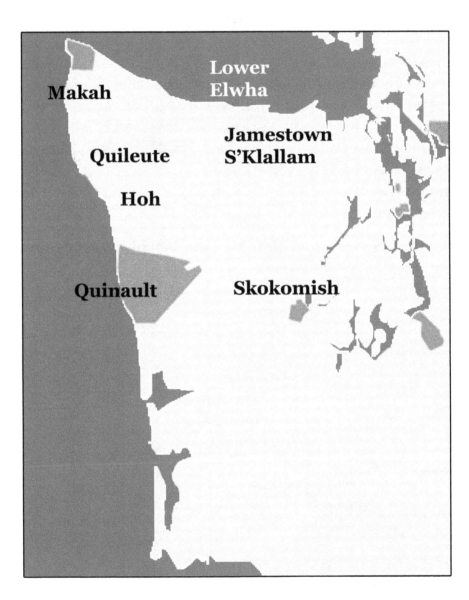

The Tribes of the Olympic Peninsula

Jamestown S'Klallam
(The Strong People)

The Jamestown S'Klallam tribe is very progressive and self-reliant. It has inhabited this area for more than 10,000 years. In 1874, when asked to move to a reservation, they refused. (Reservation: an area of land set aside by the U.S. Government for occupation by Native Americans) Instead, the Jamestown S'Klallam Tribe used $500 in gold coins to purchase 210 acres along the Strait of Juan de Fuca. The area is now called Jamestown.

Totem poles have long been used to share the rich history of the Jamestown S'Klallam People and tribes throughout the Northwest.

The Jamestown People create totem poles at S'Klallam House of Myths Carving Shed located in Sequim.

Power tools are only used to prepare logs for carving. The actual carving of the poles is done in the traditional way using only hand tools. It takes six months to a year to carve a pole from old-growth Western Red Cedar.

When I visited the carving shed, which is something you can also do, I asked why it is called the "House of Myths."

The very nice carver said, "Well, Markus, that's what we do here. We make myths."

Lower Elwha Klallam
(The Strong People)

The tribe lives on a 1000 acre reservation in the Lower Elwha River Valley.

In August 2003, the site of an ancient Klallam village, Tse-whit-zen, was discovered during a construction project on former tribal land. A nearly intact village site was uncovered. Hundreds of human remains and thousands of artifacts were found. The village site appears to have been occupied for nearly 2700 years by the Lower Elwha Klallam people. They lived there until the 1930s, when the federal government persuaded them to move to a reservation four miles west of there. The state has since returned 10 acres of land to the tribe and leased them another six acres.

Quinault
(People of the Quinault)

The Quinault People reside on an 189,621 acre reservation along Washington's coast. The word Quinault evolved from kwi'nail, the name of the tribe's settlement once situated at present-day Taholah. Taholah is the heart of today's Quinault Indian Nation.

The Quinault Indian Nation is a federally recognized tribe of Quinault, Queets, Quileute, Hoh, Chehalis, Chinook, and Cowlitz Peoples.

Makah — pronounced "muh-kaw" (The Generous Ones)

Many of the Makah, living on the Makah Reservation in Neah Bay, are skilled woodworkers and make their living as artists. Makah carvers sell carvings and masks to galleries, shops, and collectors throughout the world. The carvings usually tell a story.

The ancestors of the Makah Indian People used rocks and bones to carve designs and symbols onto ancient volcanic rocks. These petroglyphs of whales, sailing ships, hunters, and priests are 400 to 700 years old.

The sea was – and still is – a large part of the livelihood of the Makah. The carvings hold profound spiritual significance for them and should be respected by everyone.

Many believe the petroglyphs originally marked village boundaries. The carvings are in Forks, Washington on the Ozette Trail.

Makah is a complicated language with very long words and unusual sounds. I can teach you two words — ho' (rhymes with "go") means "yes," wiki· (pronounced wih-kee) means "no."

Those are the only two Makah words I know.

Skokomish Tribal Nation
(The Big River People)

The Skokomish Tribe was the largest of nine Twana communities. The Twana descendants live on the 8.2 square mile Skokomish Reservation, and all have become known as the Skokomish Tribe.

Today, many tribal members continue to work in the region's fishing and logging industries. In an attempt to diversify its economy, the tribe has purchased property for economic development and resource enhancement, as well as for housing. The Skokomish Tribe also operates its own salmon hatchery where they raise salmon for commercial purposes. As for traditional culture, many ceremonies not celebrated for 70 years or more were re-established during the late 1970s and early 1980s.

Hoh — Chalá·ator
(People of the Hoh River)

The Hoh Tribe relocated to an Indian Reservation at the mouth of the Hoh River after the signing of the Quinault Treaty on July 1, 1855. The reservation is home to one of the few temperate rain forests in the world. The Hoh River People are considered a band of the Quileutes, but they are recognized as a separate tribe. The Quileute language is also the language of the Hoh Tribe.

Quileute — pronounced "quill-ee-yoot"

The Quileute Tribe has lived and
hunted in this area for thousands
of years. They presently reside in
the coastal village of La Push.
Originally the tribe's land stretched
along the shores of the Pacific from
the glaciers of Mount Olympus to the rivers
of the rain forests.

With native languages around the world disappearing at
an alarming rate, the Quileute People are working very
hard to preserve their language for their descendants.

*I downloaded a list of common Quileute words
and phrases from the Internet. I practice them
with my friend Maxine Marmot. Quileute is a
complicated language. So far, Maxine and I have
learned that hac'h chi'i (pronounced similar to
hotch chee-ee) is a friendly greeting.*

*We are practicing saying it
to the other marmots in
our colony.*

Children Who are Members of the Tribal Communities

Native American Kids are just like all other kids except, THEY WERE HERE FIRST!

I'm sure someone at some time has asked you, "Where are you from, and how long have you lived here?" A Native American can honestly answer: "Here and always." Take a minute, and think about that.

Native American kids are members of sovereign tribal nations. Tribal sovereignty refers to the fact that each tribe has the right to govern itself. That means the United States Constitution recognizes tribes have pretty much the same powers as federal and state governments. They have laws, police, and services just like other small countries. However, they are also U.S. citizens and must obey American law.

Other than that, Native American kids are like all kids. They want to have friends, go to school, and have fun. They want to be loved, accepted, and respected. They want to have a best friend with whom to share secrets, and they fear rejection and hurt. All kids everywhere are much more alike than they are different.

So, that's the Olympic Peninsula as seen
through the eyes of this marmot.

I am very tired.
I think it's time for me to hibernate.

Signing off for now ,
Markus

CPSIA information can be obtained
at www.ICGtesting.com
Printed in the USA
JSHW010335190523
41932JS00006B/276